THE
LITTLE BOOK OF
COSMIC
ENERGY

LYDIA LEVINE

summersdale

THE LITTLE BOOK OF COSMIC ENERGY

Text by David Olliff

An Hachette UK Company
www.hachette.co.uk

Summersdale Publishers Ltd
Part of Octopus Publishing Group Limited
Carmelite House
50 Victoria Embankment
LONDON
EC4Y 0DZ
UK

www.summersdale.com

Printed and bound in China

ISBN: 978-1-83799-309-3

Substantial discounts on bulk quantities of Summersdale books are available to corporations, professional associations and other organizations. For details contact general enquiries: telephone: +44 (0) 1243 771107 or email: enquiries@summersdale.com.

CONTENTS

✦ INTRODUCTION ✦

Imagine if cosmic energy was visible to the naked eye. Light is a great example of energy we can see, as it streams through the universe, igniting in the hearts of stars and blazing across space to bathe the spinning planets. Our sun is one such star, providing all the energy on Earth, which bursts forth as life. Of course, only a small proportion of the life force that radiates through our planet is visible, but how would everything look if we could see all the energy there is, all at once?

The first thing we would notice is that there are no gaps. Even in the coldest, darkest space, there is energy. In this continuous, nearly infinite sea of light there would be countless energy centres; living creatures with radiating auras. These beings would move in and out of each other's auras, giving and receiving light in continuous transactions. All that is, or ever has been, would exist within this sea without a shore, rippling with illuminated waves.

This is cosmic energy: the energy that flows through and between us, giving us life and enabling us to flourish.

The following chapters are all about realizing our true nature as pure energy and living in harmony as part of this vast cosmic force. In Chapter One, we discover the streams of living intensity that make up our being, including the energies we receive and those we send out to others. In Chapter Two, we learn about the "energy body" and its centres, which influence our well-being in mind, body and spirit. In Chapter Three, we find tips and tricks to raise our energy vibration towards higher consciousness, better connection and happier living. And in Chapter Four, we learn how to work in harmony with cosmic energy so that we can invite health, success and happiness into our lives.

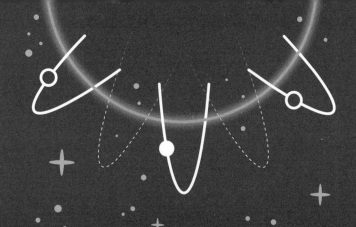

CHAPTER ONE:

THE ENERGY OF THE UNIVERSE

How would you describe your energy? Are you calm or lively, drained or overwhelmed, balanced or reactive, introspective or open-hearted?

In this chapter, we will explore the nature of the energies that make up our being. As energies flow through and from us, they have a profound impact on all aspects of life, including our motivation, enthusiasm, relationships, self-confidence, success and happiness. Healthy cosmic energy begins with being in touch with our energy streams, sensing how they make us feel and realizing how we relate to them. Energy awareness is the first step to living in cosmic harmony and flourishing in life.

✦ WHAT IS ENERGY? ✦

Back in high school you probably learned about energy in a science class, but have you ever considered that everything you discovered in this broader subject was related to energy? In physics, you might have come across potential and kinetic types, meaning that which is stored and released. You might have learned about electromagnetic energy waves and their spectrum of frequency, ranging from low-energy radio waves to high-energy gamma rays. This spectrum includes visible frequencies of light, from red to violet, and the invisible light of infrared and ultraviolet.

It wasn't just physics classes that were all about energy, however. In chemistry, you might have come across elements and compounds, from acids to explosives, including the chemical energy of fossil fuels and the radioactive energy of uranium and plutonium. In biology, you would have studied the energy of life, from photosynthesis, which allows plants to convert sunlight to food, to the bioluminescence that enables some sea creatures to glow. Simply rubbing your hands together will generate heat, which is possible because of the energy in your body, coming from calories you have consumed.

Energy is literally everywhere and everything. And this leads us to a key energy principle you may remember from school: energy cannot be created or destroyed, only converted. It can be stored, transferred or dissipated, but it never dies. Lively, flowing energy is energy undergoing conversion. Consider the flow of water rushing down the riverbed and into the sea. This is a dynamic exchange caused by gravity, itself brought on by the spinning heart of our planet.

When we discuss cosmic energy, we are talking about this same universal force, underpinned by the scientific principle that everything that exists is energy in some form. This includes physical substance or matter, and our own bodies.

✦ COSMIC STARLIGHT ✦

Energy is constantly streaming through the universe. Each of the innumerable stars scattered across space are massive concentrations of cosmic energy, which radiates over vast distances, some of it reaching us as starlight in the night sky. The stars are distant suns and their light is the visible part of the electromagnetic force bursting from them.

Stars are formed in swirling clouds of dust and gas stretching over hundreds of light years. As tiny particles the size of worlds begin to accumulate, the pressure of gravity on energy-rich gas triggers fusion and a new star detonates.

All the energy on our planet comes to us as starlight from our sun. As the sun's energy floods the Earth, plants absorb the light, trees stretch out to receive it, vegetation sprawls over the land, and in the oceans, microbial life depends on it. In this way, starlight forms the building blocks of all living things.

★ THE ENERGY OF LIFE ★

During summer, all life courses with cosmic energy. The trees are in full leaf, the grasses are tall and flowers burst with colour. Picture a hare in the early evening sun, cautiously chewing on grass – eyes watchful, ears twitching. As the hare eats, she takes in energy from the grass through a series of chemical processes. The sun's energy has been stored in the grass, and now it will be released into the bloodstream of the hare.

The complex being of this creature, from watchful eye to twitching ear, has been formed from cosmic energy. It all began as a cell in her mother's womb – a cell containing this same energy, accumulated from starlight. The hare, just like human beings and all creatures, is now the living form of energy passed from generation to generation in an unbroken chain. Now, there is potential energy stored in her powerful hind legs as she senses a fox. In a similar way, cosmic energy helps us to thrive and survive, which we will explore further in the coming chapters.

✦ THE RHYTHMS OF LIFE ✦

The fox that pursues the hare is its own form of cosmic energy from starlight. Its heart beats a pulse that regulates the flow of its life force. This same heart has kept pace with the rhythms of the living creature without fail since its first movements in the womb. It has slowed while the fox digests a meal or sleeps during the day, and quickened for the chase when a pheasant or rabbit is nearby. Now it beats lightly as the fox edges forward with tiny movements, focused intently on its prey.

All life experiences cosmic energy in rhythms, often governed by the cycles of the sun. Circadian rhythms are the natural energy cycles most animals experience over the course of a day – they're what make us wake up or feel sleepy at similar times. With the cycle of seasons, plant energy manifests as new growth or concentrates into the seed, ready to begin again.

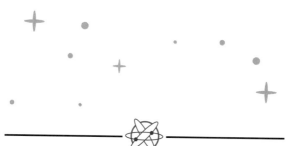

✦ WE ARE STARLIGHT ✦

As mammals, the fox and the hare are complex life forms that have evolved to consume cosmic energy from food. The hare eats vegetation, which is starlight transformed into matter. The fox, if it is quick, will make a meal of the hare. That meal would release the stored energy of starlight into the bloodstream of the fox, pumped by the rhythm of her heart.

As highly evolved life forms, we too depend on the stored energy of starlight to exist and grow. We started life as a cell with its own energy, which powered our first heartbeat. We exist now as the culmination of a chain of living energy reaching back to the first moments of life on Earth. The energy that triggered this life came from the starlight of the sun. As living beings, all that we are is this energy, whether it is stored as matter or actively flowing through us. We are, quite literally, starlight.

★ EINSTEIN'S UNIVERSE ★

These days every school student learns $E = mc^2$.

In Albert Einstein's famous formula, "E" stands for energy, "m" for mass and "c" for the speed of light. Without worrying too much about detail, this formula makes for a fascinating realization: everything that exists in the universe is energy. Everything from our physical bodies to planets has mass, or weight. According to the formula, mass represents an incredible resource of stored power.

Picture for a moment your whole being as pure energy, with no distinction between your mind, body or spirit. Then imagine the whole universe and everything in it as energy. Now think of yourself as light, in a universe also made of light, moving at such a speed that you are instantaneously everywhere all at once. This is to remind you that you are more than just your physical body; you are made of the same energy that comprises the entire cosmos.

⭐ THE COSMIC ENERGY FIELD ⭐

Over the last few decades, research in quantum physics has begun to show evidence of an interconnected cosmic energy field, as documented in Lynne McTaggart's 2003 book *The Field*. This energy field is known as the "Zero Point Field" because it is proof of energy even in the freezing vacuum of supposedly empty space. Quantum physicists have shown that the vacuum, or nothingness, does not exist. Instead, subatomic particles continue to flicker in and out of existence, exchanging energy with each other.

These findings not only support the fact that everything in the universe is pure energy, but also that everything exists within an unbroken energy field. Without any gaps, everything that exists, or has ever existed, is more like a ripple on a pond or a wave in the ocean. The Persian poet Rumi put it like this: "You are not a drop in the ocean, you are the entire ocean in a drop."

✦ FEEL THE LIVING FORCE ✦

Before we go further in our cosmic journey, let's feel the flow for ourselves.

Put your hands out in front of you, with your palms facing each other. Your hands should be around 12 inches apart, your arms in a comfortable position, with your elbows at your sides.

Place your awareness in the space between your hands. Try to relax and begin to sense the energy that is building up between your palms. Give it a little time and then gently move your hands closer together – no more than an inch or so. Allow your hands to be pushed back ever so slightly by the energy in between. Now shift your attention to the centre of your palms and notice the tingling and warm sensations, which can feel like they are radiating out to the back of your hands.

After a short time, the energy building up can begin to feel rounded like a ball. You can trace the ball's energy by gently moving your hands around its shape, bringing your palms together and allowing them to be gently pushed back.

Focus on the warm, tender and peaceful energy that has gathered in this space. When you are ready, slowly turn your hands inward towards your heart. Take some deep, slow breaths as you move your hands onto your heart. Sense the energy you have accumulated moving into your heart, bringing warmth and peace. Take three deep breaths, focus, and allow the energy to bring you a sense of calm.

If this exercise doesn't seem to work for you first time, try rubbing your hands together briskly for around a minute before trying again. Generating warmth between your hands can help to get the energy flowing.

✦ DIVINE COSMIC ENERGY ✦

The idea that human beings are made up of divine or supernatural energy is expressed in various ways in spiritual and religious thought. Different traditions and cultures use their own ideas and images to refer to the flow of energy through our natural ecosystem. *Shakti* is the primordial cosmic energy, represented by the goddess Shakti, within Hindu cultures. *Prana* is the life force often associated with the sun in yoga. *Qi*, or *chi*, is the vital energy or force connected with the breath in Taoist thought. In Christian tradition, the same divine energy flowing through a person might be referred to as the Holy Spirit.

All these different spiritual traditions point to a very similar idea: what gives life is a vibrant energy that flows through the whole being without distinction between mind, body and spirit. Mastering this energy is key to realizing our true nature as connected beings within one universal cosmic flow.

✦ LIVING ENERGY STREAMS ✦

How would you describe your cosmic energy levels right now? There are lots of ways of thinking about our own cosmic energy: health and wellness, enthusiasm and motivation, our sense of liveliness of spirit or our get-up-and-go. This relates to our emotional state – our moods and feelings, so often influenced by relationships with others. Our cosmic energy also depends on how we see ourselves, our confidence and sense of self-belief. We also need to consider how connected we feel to the energies around us, our willingness to trust in life's path and our openness to regenerative influences, success and prosperity.

With these aspects of our lives in mind, it can be helpful to think of our energy as four separate but closely intertwined streams. These streams can be identified as active energy, responsive, reflective and receptive energy. We will find out more about each of these over the next few pages.

✦ YOUR ACTIVE ENERGY STREAM ✦

Your active energy stream relates to your well-being, and maintains your mental and physical health, including strength, motivation, enthusiasm, purpose and liveliness of spirit.

When your active energy stream is blocked, you may feel unwell or experience other physical symptoms. You might be more tired or lethargic than usual, lack motivation or find yourself unable to focus. Sometimes your active energy stream can be too active, leaving you overwhelmed and indecisive, struggling to keep all the plates spinning at once.

When these energies are flowing, you will feel well, you will have a clear sense of purpose and be able to focus in the moment with minimal distraction. You might feel a sense of excitement and positivity, ready to seize the day and meet the challenges of life head on. Remember those times when you're in the zone? Psychologists call this flow, when your active energies are just right and you're unstoppable!

★ YOUR RESPONSIVE ENERGY STREAM ★

Your responsive energy stream relates to your sense of contentment, emotional state and moods. It primarily concerns your relationships with others but it is also about how you relate to events and situations as they arise in your life.

When your responsive energy stream is blocked, you become more reactive than responsive. This tends to lead to a spikey emotional state, up one minute and down the next, depending on the most recent interaction with another person. You might find yourself lurching from one crisis to the next without any sense of control.

When these energies are flowing well, you experience your emotions in a more balanced and manageable way. Our emotional life can feel like we're sailing a tiny boat on a vast ocean, whether it be choppy, dead calm, rough seas or with a storm brewing on the horizon. When your responsive energies are flowing well, you sail the same unpredictable waters but with the confidence of a calm and steady navigator.

★ YOUR REFLECTIVE ENERGY STREAM ★

Your reflective energy stream relates to self-actualization. This is about how you see yourself, your identity and your authenticity. Your reflective energy concerns the relationship between the person you are and the person you think you should be. It is about self-knowledge and the discovery of your true nature.

When your reflective energy stream is blocked, you may have low self-esteem and a general sense of unworthiness. You might struggle to fit in, find it hard to believe that others care for you, or place others on a pedestal while you dwell on your failings and mistakes. An excess in reflective energy can be self-limiting, in the sense that one can become too self-obsessed, thinking only about oneself.

When these energies are flowing, you feel confident and self-assured, comfortable in your own skin, which creates resilience. You can forgive yourself your flaws and love who you are.

✦ YOUR RECEPTIVE ENERGY STREAM ✦

Your receptive energy stream relates to success and prosperity. It is about manifestation, making your goals and dreams a reality, and attracting wealth in every sense of the word.

If your receptive energy stream is blocked, you might build up an expectation of disappointment. You might approach every challenge with a negative outlook and come to believe that things only work out for other people. This cynicism can lead to a competitive mindset, where it seems that wealth is only achieved at the expense of others.

When these energies are flowing well, you have faith in divine abundance (a state that is not diminishable, with nothing lacking) and confidence in providence (the protective care of nature – or a god – as a spiritual power). You feel able to trust in the limitlessness of cosmic energy and know that the universe is on your side. You are open to prosperity, knowing that you have only to ask in order to receive. You welcome good fortune and look forward to positive outcomes. Thankfulness and a spirit of gratitude accompany this energy stream.

✸ HAPPINESS AND HARMONY ✸

Our cosmic energy is our vital life force. It radiates from a core within us and reaches out in interactions with the beings that surround us. Our active and reflective energies are internal to us, while our responsive and receptive energies constantly exchange flow with the beings and forces outside of us.

While it is a central principle of cosmic energy that everything is connected, it is also true to say that the cosmic energy within which we live exists as dynamic waves and constantly vibrating particles, all interacting with each other. As concentrations of this energy, each one of us is living in a relationship of constant giving and receiving with the energy that surrounds us, influenced as it is by other people, who are energy centres just like us.

This thinking has implications for the way we choose to live. Realizing that we are beings of light means that happiness and fulfilment are to be found in harmony with the cosmos and all other beings.

Aristotle used the word "flourishing" to describe a life well lived; we can choose to flourish within the limitless sea of cosmic energy. Thinking of our energy as four streams is a highly effective guide, and each of these can be thought of as having a goal for the flourishing self:

★ Your active energy stream seeks wellness and inspiration.
★ Your responsive energy stream seeks love and contentment.
★ Your reflective energy stream seeks inner peace and self-actualization.
★ Your receptive energy stream seeks fruitfulness and prosperity.

As we progress through this guide, you will find plenty of techniques to open up each of these streams for an abundant and positive flow. The good news is that as you work on one stream, you support all the others, and therefore can ultimately achieve energy harmony.

✦ HARMONIZING YOUR ENERGIES ✦

Living well as an "energy being" is all about harmony. Our four energy streams are so interdependent that in order to harmonize as one, they must feed off and receive from each other.

Suppose you feel blocked in your receptive energies. "Good things never come easily to me," you might tell yourself. This cynicism will also block your responsive energies as your interactions with others become just a little muted and downbeat. You might miss the chance to encourage someone else: "I wouldn't get your hopes up", you might find yourself saying.

What you say to others, you are really saying to yourself. This will block your reflective energies because the despondency will turn inwards. Deep down, you will know you missed a chance to share positive energy with another, and this will, in turn, dampen your self-esteem. With these accumulating blockages, your active energy will flatten, leaving you without much in the way of enthusiasm or motivation.

However, realizing that our energy streams are connected is also the key to reversing negative energy cycles. All you have to do is work on one area to set up a kind of feedforward spiral, which will naturally amplify and enhance your whole self.

If you're ever stuck, start with your responsive energies; find every chance you can to inspire, encourage and support someone else. This will generate positivity that will surround and influence you, too. Your reflective energy stream will be enhanced as you come to see yourself in a more positive light, which will in turn boost your receptive energy. As you start to welcome good things for yourself and others, you will become more tuned in to your true potential, enriching your active energy.

Often all it takes is one small change to trigger a positive energy cycle away from self-limitation and towards self-flourishing.

✦ ENERGY HEALING ✦

We all exist as energy centres in reciprocal relationships with one another, giving and receiving in a constant flow, even when we are not consciously aware of doing so. This means we are able to support each other in achieving a more positive, higher-frequency vibration.

When our cosmic energies are blocked, particularly if this is manifesting as illness or lethargy, we might find we struggle to access the internal resources necessary to restore ourselves. That's when an energy healer can make a difference. An energy healer is someone who is particularly adept at sensing energy flow and acting to restore energy harmony. They can identify the source of a block and help to clear it, effectively reversing a draining cycle.

There are a range of energy-healing techniques, including reiki, chakra healing and crystal-based healing. All of them seek to revive and balance energy flow towards wellness and realignment with cosmic abundance.

Reiki

Reiki is a Japanese healing practice founded in the early twentieth century. It works by channelling the unseen life force that flows through everything. During a session, a reiki practitioner will place their hands lightly above or on your body to encourage healing. You can give yourself a full reiki self-treatment at home, by laying your hands on one of your chakras – which you will read more about in the next chapter – for 3–5 minutes. As you do it, imagine you are encouraging universal life-force energy through your hands.

Crystal healing

Crystals have been used as a healing tool for centuries. Different types of crystal are thought to have their own unique energies, and it is believed that they can heal physical, emotional and spiritual aspects of ourselves. Crystals can be used for energy healing by placing them on your chakras with the aim of encouraging the invisible life-force energy to flow freely – see page 55 to find out which crystals are best for which chakras.

★ WHAT DO WE MEAN BY VIBRATIONS? ★

You are a living energy field composed of energy-producing particles, each of which is in perpetual motion. So, like every energy being in the cosmos, you are constantly vibrating and creating energy.

Vibrations are a kind of rhythm. Your heartbeat, breathing and circadian rhythms are those that you can see, feel and measure. But there are also smaller vibrations, such as the molecules within your cells.

Vibrational medicine is a practice that seeks ways to use and influence the energy you generate in order to improve your overall well-being.

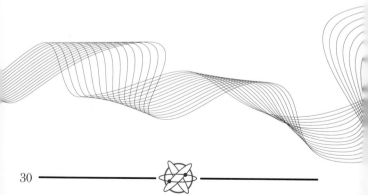

Raising your vibration

Vibrating at a higher frequency means stretching out to the full extent of your energy being and reaching towards a higher level of consciousness, so that you can live a happier and healthier life. This can be achieved through meditation, visualization and other well-being-boosting activities (see Chapter Three), although often the key to raising your vibration lies in mindful awareness and openness.

Our whole being consists of an energy spectrum, from the densest, lowest frequency, which is our physical body, to the most ethereal, highest frequency of pure consciousness. In Chapter Two, you will see how our energy is distributed across different frequencies, while Chapter Three has ideas to raise your vibration towards a higher frequency.

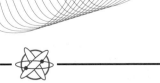

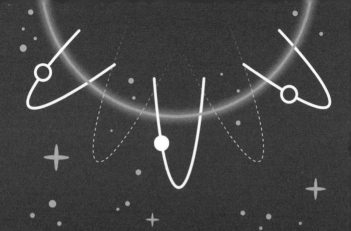

CHAPTER TWO:

COSMIC ENERGY, CHAKRAS AND AURAS

In this chapter, we explore the energy body and discover the seven energy centres of the self, known as chakras, which regulate and channel energy flow. We also discover how the energy body radiates beyond the physical form as an aura made up of seven layers or bodies of light.

We will learn the importance of maintaining the energy body in order to achieve wellness, energy harmony and, ultimately, a flourishing life. We also discover tools and techniques to balance and optimize our chakras, and to ensure a healthy aura that is clear, bright and free of negative influences.

✦ YOUR CHAKRAS AND ENERGY FLOW ✦

Chakra is a Sanskrit word meaning "circle" or "wheel". Essentially, chakras can be thought of as energy centres or vortexes in the body. The spiritual teaching of chakras can be traced back to sacred Hindu texts, known as the *Vedas*, which originated in India between 1200 and 200 BCE.

Chakras act like distribution centres, radiating cosmic energy via a network of channels throughout the body. In yoga practice, cosmic energy is focused particularly on the life energy known as *prana*. Prana is said to flow through thousands of these subtle channels. As major junctions in this system, the chakras are seven central conduits, which run down the spine of the physical body.

Each chakra has a specific vibration, from the low frequency of the physical body to the highest frequency of the true, spiritual self. If our cosmic energy is to flow effectively through our whole being, our chakras must be kept open, balanced, bright and clear.

✦ SPINNING WHEELS OF COSMIC ENERGY ✦

Our chakras are constantly spinning, vibrating wheels of living energy. These centres make up the energy self: the physical body and the other layers of the energy field. The seven chakras run from the base of the spine all the way up to the top of the head, and each are associated with a different – but connected – aspect of our cosmic energy.

Chakras distribute and regulate cosmic energy, bringing together our physical, mental, emotional and spiritual bodies. Our chakras therefore influence and reflect how we feel in terms of physical and mental wellness, emotional stability or spiritual consciousness. When our chakras are balanced, we can expect energetic harmony, with a healthy and even energy flow throughout our whole being; we feel generous of spirit, confident and aligned with divine abundance. In short, we flourish.

✦ THE SEVEN CHAKRAS ✦

From the base of the spine up to the crown of the head, each of the seven chakras is associated with a vibration and an aspect of our living energy. Each chakra is also represented by a colour of the light spectrum, from lower-frequency red light to higher-frequency violet light.

The Root Chakra
Colour: Red
Sanskrit Name: Muladhara
Meaning: The solid core
Location: Base of the spine

The Sacral Chakra
Colour: Orange
Sanskrit Name: Svadhisthana
Meaning: The place of the self
Location: The pelvic region, 2 inches below the navel

The Solar Plexus Chakra

Colour: Yellow
Sanskrit Name: Manipura
Meaning: The lustrous gem
Location: In the stomach, 2 inches above the navel

The Heart Chakra

Colour: Green
Sanskrit Name: Anahata
Meaning: The unhurt
Location: In the centre of the chest

The Throat Chakra

Colour: Sky Blue
Sanskrit Name: Vishuddha
Meaning: Essence of purity
Location: In the middle of the throat

The Third Eye Chakra
Colour: Indigo
Sanskrit Name: Ajna
Meaning: Beyond wisdom
Location: Between the eyebrows

The Crown Chakra
Colour: Violet or White
Sanskrit Name: Sahasrara
Meaning: A thousand petals
Location: At the top of the head,
just on the crown

✦ THE ROOT CHAKRA ✦

The root chakra is located at the bottom of the spine, towards the perineum for men or the cervical area for women. It can be sensed at the tip of the tail bone or the front of the pubic bone.

Our root chakra connects the energy of our physical body with the energy of the Earth itself, channelling grounding energy down through the feet. It is associated with the survival instinct – our need for safety, security, shelter and sustenance.

When we are open to universal abundance, our primary needs are met. This is why the root chakra is concerned with basic trust and sure faith: trust in our own true nature and faith that the universe will provide for all our needs. When our root chakra is clear and bright, our reflective energies can flow freely into our receptive energies, welcoming self-confidence, stability and prosperity.

★ THE SACRAL CHAKRA ★

The sacral chakra is located about 2 inches below the navel. It can be sensed just under the waistline, around 2 inches inside the body.

Our sacral chakra is physically connected with our sexual organs, primarily the ovaries or testes. In this sense, the sacral chakra channels energies of reproduction, renewal, generation and fertility. It is associated with our passions, sexuality, creativity and desires.

To experience this energy, reflect for a moment on your emotions when you have encountered true beauty. Feel that sense of yearning and the creative responses it awakens. When our sacral chakra is clear and bright, our active energies can flow freely into our responsive energies, welcoming inspiration, passion and love.

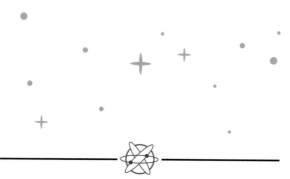

✦ SOLAR PLEXUS CHAKRA ✦

The solar plexus chakra is located about 2 inches above the navel. It can be sensed in the stomach region.

Our solar plexus chakra is physically connected with our stomach and digestive system. The solar plexus chakra channels energy from our major energy source: the food we eat. This means our feelings and behaviours around food are stored in this chakra. It is also associated with our power force, our assertiveness and decisiveness.

There is a connection with energy conversion both in the sense of food, which is converted to energy, and willpower. Willpower is all about the conversion of energy. Our ideas, dreams and creative inspirations begin as energy, which is in turn brought into being by action and willpower. This is how we manifest our desires and turn them into reality. When our solar plexus chakra is clear and bright, our active energies can flow freely into our receptive energies, welcoming inspiration brought to manifestation.

★ THE HEART CHAKRA ★

The heart chakra is located in the centre of the chest, near the heart. It can be sensed in the middle of the breastbone, a few inches inside the body.

Our heart chakra is physically connected with our heart organ. Being the central point between our lower and higher chakras, our heart chakra connects the physical self with the spiritual self. The lower chakras concern our physical needs and desires, while the upper chakras look at our spiritual consciousness, intuition and intellect.

We may know the pain of a heart broken apart, but there is true beauty in a heart broken open. Our heart chakra is associated with love, compassion, kindness and empathy expressed as open-heartedness towards others, but also towards ourselves; this invites generosity, forgiveness, patience and understanding. When our heart chakra is clear and bright, our responsive energies can flow freely into our reflective energies, welcoming love, contentment and inner peace.

✦ THE THROAT CHAKRA ✦

The throat chakra is located in the middle of the throat and can be sensed in the lower half of the neck, below the Adam's apple.

Our throat chakra is physically connected with our throat, larynx and thyroid gland. The thyroid gland is itself an energy regulator, as it stores hormones that govern body temperature and the rate at which food is converted into energy. Our throat chakra is associated with communication, truth and integrity.

Communication is an energy all of its own. The words we speak not only carry resonance as sound waves, they also have a powerful impact on others and on ourselves. Our throat chakra concerns the power of language to support, encourage, transform and heal. It also concerns the purpose of language, which is to speak truth with integrity. When our throat chakra is clear and bright, our responsive energies can flow freely into our reflective energies, welcoming generosity of spirit, personal integrity and kind words.

✦ THE THIRD EYE CHAKRA ✦

The third eye chakra is located between the eyebrows and can be sensed just a little above the brow line in the centre of the lower forehead.

Our third eye chakra is physically connected with our mind and eyes. It is the meeting point between intellect and intuition, and can be thought of as two complementary energies: understanding, which is related to intelligence and comprehension; and wisdom, which is related to intuition and good judgement. Working in harmony, these energies reveal insight and knowledge.

Our third eye chakra is all about seeing the truth. This includes insights into our true nature as a living being and also of divine oneness. When intuition comes to us it feels like a new kind of knowing: suddenly we see clearly. This is the vision of the third eye. When our third eye chakra is clear and bright, our active energies are flowing freely into our reflective energies, welcoming revelation, self-knowledge and true insight.

✦ THE CROWN CHAKRA ✦

The crown chakra is located at the top of the head. It can be sensed just above the head, almost like it is being worn as a crown, but its centre is higher up.

Our crown chakra is within our energy field but not connected with our physical body. It is a bright energy of intense light, often sensed as stark white with a violet outline. It is associated with spiritual enlightenment and oneness and is our connection to the divine.

This chakra concerns the divine light within all of us. In individuals who have achieved enlightenment, it is alleged that the divine light has been seen to radiate from the crown of the head, which may be the inspiration for halos depicted around saints and other holy figures. When our crown chakra is clear and bright, our active energies flow freely into our receptive energies, welcoming inspiration, manifestation and prosperity.

★ BLOCKED CHAKRAS ★

Our seven chakras are conduits for cosmic energy and, like any channel, they can become blocked or unstable. Negative energies are easily accumulated in daily life; we absorb all the cynicism and distrust, stresses and pressures, and fears and anxieties that surround us. These come from a range of sources. Remember that we live as energy centres constantly interacting with other energy beings, so the way in which others behave around us, the language they use and the thoughts and feelings they dwell on will inevitably flow to us.

In addition, our own self-limiting thoughts and reactions to life events can have a negative impact on our energies. These negative influences behave like toxins. They build up slowly so that in time we feel unstable, unwell, out of balance, ill at ease, distrustful, anxious or unable to make progress. There are ways to unblock chakras, however, and we will explore this in more detail in the coming pages.

✦ CHAKRA CLEANSING ✦

Our mental, spiritual and physical health depends on the positive and balanced circulation of cosmic energy throughout the body. It is so important to take care of our chakras, to ensure they remain free-flowing conduits for life-affirming energy.

Chakra-based healing entails tuning into our chakras in order to identify what needs healing in our lives. Chakra work can help us get to the root of any imbalance, disconnectedness or illness we might be experiencing. Discovering the root cause of blockages, which prevent us from flourishing, is the first step to renewal, rejuvenation and healing.

Cleansing chakras involves clearing out old energies that have led to stagnation and nourishing the energetic body, leaving us refreshed and recharged. Chakra cleansing work is all about listening to your body, determining what feels blocked, and opening the self to regenerative influences.

✦ CLEANSING THE ROOT CHAKRA ✦

When the root chakra becomes blocked, we find ourselves worrying. We become anxious that we do not have enough, that we are unsafe or under threat. We might generate fears about future financial security and the stability of our homes. We lose sleep fretting about our vulnerability to the uncertainties of life.

Physically, this might lead to digestive problems or overwhelming feelings of stress and general anxiety.

Essential for countering these fears is realizing the difference between experiencing loss and fearing loss. Loss is a fact of life and vulnerability is unavoidable at times. When the root chakra is blocked, it is an exaggerated fear of loss that results, even if the actual risk is quite low.

To unblock the root chakra, seek grounding experiences such as walking in woodland or gratitude journaling to help you reconnect with abundance. Manage your anxiety with mindfulness practices to keep you rooted in the present. Fear, after all, is usually fixated on the future.

✦ CLEANSING THE SACRAL CHAKRA ✦

When the sacral chakra becomes blocked, it may manifest as a lack of creativity. This in turn can cause frustration, leaving us unable to find inspiration or the motivation to get things done. Self-esteem will suffer too as we struggle to like ourselves.

Physically, this might flatten the libido and lead to difficulties with sexual intimacy or satisfaction.

Sometimes blockages here might simply be caused by the routine of the daily grind. It is all too easy to get stuck in repetitive, unvaried patterns in life and work activity. Routines can be comforting, but enthusiasm relies on having something fresh to look forward to.

To counter these feelings, try a little self-indulgence, such as a pampering experience, or taking the time to prepare a different meal with a lively range of flavours. Release your inner artist by working with bright colours as freely as possible; just try to let go and express yourself.

✦ CLEANSING THE
SOLAR PLEXUS CHAKRA ✦

When the solar plexus chakra becomes blocked, we experience a sense of powerlessness. We might have difficulty moving forward, and struggle to put plans into action. This can manifest as indecisiveness, fear of commitment, a feeling of inadequacy or a lack of self-confidence.

Physically, this might lead to weight issues or the development of disordered eating habits.

Blockages in this area build up when we experience helplessness and become overwhelmed by the relentless challenges of life. Too often it seems like other people cope better than we do, although it's important to remember that we cannot possibly know how they feel on the inside.

To counter these feelings, take note of the thoughts you have about yourself – each day, find something to like. Congratulate yourself for something done well; reframe your self-talk with encouragement and kindness. Try some positive affirmations throughout your day, which can be powerfully enhanced through EFT tapping (see page 88 on the Emotional Freedom Technique).

✦ CLEANSING THE
HEART CHAKRA ✦

When the heart chakra becomes blocked, we feel hurt – a common emotion arising from our interactions with others. The hurt might come from the way we have been treated by a partner, a parent, a friend, our own children or a colleague. When the heart aches, there is a terrible sense of loss, grief and sadness. It may be the hurt arises from loss of a loved one through death or separation. Heartache and heartbreak are true and valid feelings, which we all must go through from time to time. Experiencing such emotions is not what blocks the heart chakra – it is being unable to release them and let them go in their proper time.

To counter these feelings, give freely and reach out in love to others whenever possible, and try to forgive those who cause you hurt. It might feel impossible, but any forgiveness, love or kindness you can show will begin the process of heart healing.

★ CLEANSING THE THROAT CHAKRA ★

When the throat chakra becomes blocked, we struggle to communicate effectively. We might find it difficult to express what we really feel, to share our emotions or to reveal our true selves. This can manifest as anxiety concerning speaking up for ourselves, because we are afraid of what others might think of us. As a result, we will tend to hide behind different personas.

Physically, this might lead to a sore throat, recurrent acid reflux or struggles with a sense of identity.

To counter these feelings, try using a journal to regularly express your feelings. It could be that poetry might prove a useful form of expression to help you find your voice. Discovering your true self by writing with honesty will develop self-knowledge, which is the first step to living authentically. Having someone you trust who will listen without judgement can be immensely valuable. Talk things over and share your feelings with a trusted friend and try to be the friend who listens too.

✦ CLEANSING THE THIRD EYE CHAKRA ✦

When the third eye chakra becomes blocked, we struggle with knowledge and certainty. We might find it difficult to discern truth, form sound judgements or achieve balance. For this reason, it can be difficult to know when our perspective is skewed. A blockage in this area might manifest itself in persistent doubt and uncertainty, leading to a lack of confidence. Equally, it could result in poor judgement, leading to an unsound conviction of being right when we're actually wrong.

Physically, this may cause headaches and migraines, as well as difficulty with clarity.

Guard against problems in this area through humility; extreme and polarized opinions rarely reveal truth. Listen more than you're used to and take time to see any alternative point of view. If you're overthinking things, try to meditate mindfully each day and focus on the breath, while letting go of intrusive thoughts. Not everything in life is a problem requiring a solution; sometimes it's OK to just be.

✦ CLEANSING THE CROWN CHAKRA ✦

The crown chakra is all about the divine. The divine will mean different things to different people, but in the end, it is for each of us individually to discern what, or who, we come to rely on. For some, faith in the divine is so absolute they live as though faith is certainty, while others put more emphasis on themselves, or on material things such as food, money or even their mobile phone. Blockages in the crown chakra create distrust in divine abundance and over-reliance on the self. A blockage in this area can lead to compulsive behaviour, excessive accumulation of wealth, obsessiveness, overachieving or overwork.

Physically, this will likely lead to stress and anxiety, as no material thing can offer true security. To counter these concerns, find time each day to sit still and do nothing. Try a detox to release over-reliance: perhaps a digital detox or a refreshing declutter (see page 96).

★ CHAKRA-HEALING TOOLS ★

Each chakra is, in essence, an energy centre of its own, with its individual signature. Inviting influences into our environment that reflect or stimulate this can be a helpful way to open up our chakras and encourage positive energy circulation. Some ideas for chakra-healing influences could include burning a particular incense, lighting a candle or lamp, using a few drops of an essential oil in a room spray or bath, or carrying one of the crystals with you.

Root Chakra
Candle or Lamp: Red
Crystals: Haematite, obsidian, moss agate
Incense: Cedar
Essential Oil: Patchouli

Sacral Chakra
Candle or Lamp: Orange
Crystals: Tiger's Eye, citrine, moonstone
Incense: Rose
Essential Oil: Ylang-ylang

Solar Plexus Chakra
Candle or Lamp: Yellow
Crystals: Agate, pyrite, amber, sunstone
Incense: Sandalwood
Essential Oil: Rosemary

Heart Chakra
Candle or Lamp: Green or pink
Crystals: rose quartz, (green) jade, green calcite
Incense: Jasmine
Essential Oil: Eucalyptus

Throat Chakra
Candle or Lamp: Light blue or turquoise
Crystals: Blue lace agate, aquamarine, turquoise
Incense: Frankincense
Essential Oil: Peppermint

Third Eye Chakra

Candle or Lamp: Dark blue or purple
Crystals: Sodalite, fluorite, Lapis Lazuli
Incense: Sage
Essential Oil: Star Anise

Crown Chakra

Candle: White or violet
Crystals: Clear quartz, diamond, amethyst
Incense: Myrrh
Essential Oil: Lavender

✦ CHAKRA-HEALING AFFIRMATIONS ✦

When our chakras are blocked, clearing them and restoring energy flow can begin with positive self-talk. Often, the way we see ourselves, the way we feel about ourselves and the internal dialogues we have are significant contributors to restricted and unstable energy flow. Daily affirmations can help reframe our self-reflection and initiate a healing cycle. Here are some affirmations for each chakra to try reciting throughout your day:

Root Chakra

I am centred and grounded.
I feel safe.
The universe is on my side.

Sacral Chakra

I am a conduit for creativity and beauty.
I embrace my sexuality.
I deserve to enjoy life.

Solar Plexus Chakra

I feel my own power.
I am filled with immortal fire.
I have unlimited potential.

Heart Chakra

I forgive myself and others.
I love myself and others.
I follow the voice of my heart.

Throat Chakra

I hear and speak truth.
I am open and honest.
I live with integrity.

Third Eye Chakra

I see clearly.
I think clearly.
I know clearly.

Crown Chakra

I am one.
I am spirit.
I am divine.

✦ MEDITATION FOR CHAKRA HARMONY ✦

The most powerful technique for restoring energy flow, clearing blockages and activating your chakras is through meditation. Chakra meditation involves engaging with your chakras in turn. With each one, you begin by simply checking in. As you focus your attention on each chakra, you will awaken its energy and initialize a healing cycle in that area. This activates your stream of cosmic energy to flow more freely and generously.

How to practise chakra-harmonizing meditation:

★ Find somewhere comfortable to sit where you won't be disturbed for at least 20 minutes.

★ Many practitioners recommend a legs-folded position on the floor, but to begin with, a comfortable chair is fine. If you are seated in a chair, ensure your feet are flat on the floor. Sit upright and allow your hands to rest gently on your thighs.

★ Begin by breathing mindfully. Just be aware as you breathe deeply and slowly. Take the time to feel fully relaxed.

★ Bring your attention to your root chakra. Try to sense the energy at that location in your energy body. Visualize the root chakra in its vivid red colour. Breathe into your root chakra and as you do, visualize its light growing brighter, clearer and more intense. Begin to notice the chakra spinning in a clockwise direction. Notice the chakra clearing, cleansing and balancing.

★ When you are comfortable that your root chakra is clear, bright, balanced and spinning, move on to your sacral chakra.

★ Repeat the process for each of your chakras until they are all clear, bright and balanced in their respective colours, each the same size and spinning at the same rate.

★ With all your chakras balanced, visualize a healing stream of bright white light entering your energy body through your crown chakra. Sense this light flowing through all your chakras, then radiating throughout your energy body.

This meditation works best when practised regularly. Look online for guided chakra-cleansing meditations to support your practice.

✦ CLEANSING A SPECIFIC CHAKRA ✦

A single-chakra meditation is the best way to identify and clear blockages in a specific chakra. Perhaps you have been feeling blocked in one particular area in your life. Maybe you have been struggling to let go of feelings of betrayal and would like to work on your heart chakra.

Deciding which chakra to work with might not be obvious to you. If this is the case, work with your third eye chakra first. This will guide you to trust your intuition and help you decide the chakra that needs your attention most.

How to practise a single-chakra meditation:

★ Take inspiration from the list of chakra-healing influences above. Set up your environment to invite the energy of your chosen chakra.

★ Memorize the three healing affirmations for your chosen chakra from the previous list.

★ Note the meaning of your chosen chakra from the list at the beginning of this chapter.

★ Find somewhere to sit where you won't be disturbed for at least 20 minutes.

★ Sit in a comfortable chair and ensure your feet are flat on the floor. Sit upright and allow your hands to rest easily in your lap.

★ Close your eyes and begin to breathe mindfully. Take the time to feel fully relaxed.

★ When you are ready, recite your set of three healing affirmations seven times as a mantra, allowing for deep, relaxing breaths in between.

★ Breathe into your chosen chakra location. Really focus your attention at the location and sense the energy building. As you do this, visualize a sphere surrounding your whole body, filling more and more with the colour of your chosen chakra. Feel the intensity of this light increasing.

★ Bring to mind the meaning of your chosen chakra. Bathed in the coloured light, spend time allowing this meaning to permeate your energy being.

★ When you have finished this meditation, take time to journal any feelings, thoughts or insights that arise.

✦ THE AURA ✦

Our physical bodies represent only a part of our whole energy being. The physical body is the densest, lowest-frequency part of ourselves, while our whole energy being reaches out towards the most ethereal, highest-frequency self, which is pure consciousness. The energy of the physical body, which vibrates slowly or with the lowest frequency, is naturally perceptible to us. However, those energies of the self that vibrate more quickly or with higher frequency are beyond standard perception.

The aura is the field of energy that completely surrounds the physical body and radiates out in layers, from the lowest frequency to the highest. It is generally oval in shape, extending below the feet and above the head. With a little practice, it is possible to see the inner aura (known as the "etheric body") with the human eye. Some highly tuned individuals can see the outer aura through a developed psychic perception. The aura can also be sensed with the hands or through the use of a dowsing pendulum.

The aura is made up of seven layers, called "auric bodies". In some ways, the auric bodies are related to chakras, in that they range from lower to higher frequencies of the energy self, and they each represent an aspect of being. The auric bodies are:

* Etheric body – the lower physical aspect (physical plane – inner aura)
* Emotional body – the lower emotional aspect (physical plane)
* Mental body – the lower mental aspect (physical plane)
* Astral body – the harmonizing aspect (astral plane – the bridge)
* Etheric template – the higher physical aspect (spiritual plane – outer aura)
* Celestial body – the higher emotional aspect (spiritual plane – outer aura)
* Ketheric or causal body – the higher mental aspect (spiritual plane – outer aura)

When our energies become unstable or blocked, this can manifest in the aura. Energy-healing techniques such as reiki can cleanse the aura, while raising our vibration generally helps keep it clear and balanced. There are some specific aura-cleansing practices for you to try over the next few pages.

★ SEEING THE INNER AURA ★

With a little practice, most people find they can see the inner aura. This is the layer of the aura known as the etheric body, which very closely follows the outline of the physical extraneous spaces extending for less than an inch from the body outline and tending to be seen as a haze, with perhaps a pale blue-grey tint. The etheric body has an energy vibration that is just a little higher than the physical body, and is therefore more a part of our physical than spiritual nature. This means it can be picked up with our physical senses.

To practise seeing your own inner aura, try this exercise:

★ Put your hands comfortably out in front of you, around 12 to 16 inches where you can see your fingers well, palms facing you. The background should be a plain surface – a white wall or a sheet of plain paper.

★ Line up the four fingers of each hand so that they are almost touching. Now relax your eyes and try not to focus on your fingers. In time, you should begin to see the trace of a faint outline around your fingers. Eventually, the outline will seem to extend.

★ This may seem like a trick of the light, except where the tips of your fingers nearly meet. Where the outlines penetrate each other, try slowly and carefully moving your fingers apart. Many people notice that the aura stretches a little between the fingers before separating into outlines.

★ THE OUTER AURA ★

Our outer energy being radiates beyond the physical body as an egg-shaped aura, which in most people extends up to 5 feet from the physical outline. This outer aura is made up of layers, or auric bodies, with a much higher energy vibration than the physical body so only highly sensitive, psychically attuned people can perceive it.

The size of our aura can expand or contract depending on a range of factors such as our emotional state or our mental and physical health. Highly spiritually developed people have been said to have auras of 30 feet or more! The colour and clarity of our aura is also subject to change due to our dominant mood, environmental factors, interactions with others and, again, our mental and physical well-being. Those who are able to read the outer aura associate certain colours with aspects of our emotional state, personality and wellness:

Red: Vitality, passion, enthusiasm.
Orange: Confidence, creativity, inspiration.
Yellow: Optimism, friendliness, intellectualism.
Green: Peace, harmony, unconditional love.
Blue: Devotion, empathy, intuition.
Indigo: Spiritual awakening, calm, imagination.
Violet: Sensitive, playful, charming.
Black: Spiritually oppressed, negativity, addiction.
Grey: Depression, exhaustion, scepticism.
Silver/Gold: Divine connection, spiritually connected, enlightened.
Brown: Greed, guilt, struggling spiritually.

Seeing the outer aura doesn't come easily to most people and certainly takes patience and practice. You can make a start by trying to see a friend's or partner's aura. Ask their permission first and take your time. With relaxed eyes and gentle vision, gaze at the third eye chakra in their forehead and try to sense the periphery as you ask (in your mind) to have the aura revealed to you. If you can't see it right away, don't worry, just re-centre yourself and try again.

★ AURA CLEANSING ★

As we go about our daily lives, our whole energy being is subject to a full range of physical, environmental, emotional, mental and spiritual influences. Every interaction we have with others is an energy exchange on some level, while the energies of our surroundings can have a significant impact on our energetic harmony and overall wellness. Our auras pick up countless energy influences each day, a great many of which we hardly notice, but they can build up over time. We pass in and out of other people's auras simply walking down the street, potentially picking up their residual energies.

Cleansing your aura is a great way to sweep away any toxic energies you may have accumulated. An aura cleanse can help you release tension, let go of negative thought patterns, clear your mind and free yourself emotionally. Regular aura cleansing can help towards a healthier, happier and calmer you.

★ WHEN TO CLEANSE YOUR AURA ★

Any time is a good time to cleanse your aura and take care of your energy self. Here are some examples of when negative energies can accumulate:

★ When you get home from a busy day at work or are simply frantically trying to get everything done. An aura cleanse will help you reset for a more restful evening.

★ After any negative interactions with others. Aura cleansing can help you still your mind following arguments, disagreements or confrontations.

★ After any emotionally intense interactions with others. Cleansing your aura can help you to put aside the feelings you inevitably take on through empathy and sympathy. It is kind to share in another's loss or sadness, but also important to release those feelings.

★ Whenever you feel anxious. If you have been experiencing worry, perhaps because of an upcoming situation such as an exam or interview, an aura cleanse can smooth out your spikey energies.

✦ CLEANSE YOUR AURA WITH... ✦

Smudging

Smudging is a practice using incense smoke, which originated within Indigenous American culture. The herb white sage is most commonly preferred for aura cleansing because of its purifying properties.

In Indigenous American practice, a sage bundle, a large open shell and a feather are used. If you have these available, light the sage so that it smoulders with plenty of smoke, place it in the shell and use the feather to waft the smoke around your space and fill your aura with the purifying incense. Cedar, frankincense or myrrh are effective alternatives. Simply allow the incense to penetrate and dissipate throughout your aura and sense negative or blocked energies drifting away with the smoke.

Do take great care with incense. Use in a well-ventilated area, consider possible allergies and be aware that a smouldering sage bundle can be a fire risk, so always extinguish carefully.

A blissful bath

A soak in the bath is the perfect remedy for most of life's stresses and strains. Bathing in essential oils, purifying bath salts and energizing crystals will literally wash away negative energies and unhelpful emotional residues from your aura.

First, run a comfortably warm bath and add a generous cupful of purifying salt – Epsom salts or Himalayan rock salt are perfect. Add a few drops of a favourite aura-cleansing essential oil such as lavender or eucalyptus. As you do so, maintain a clear intention in your mind to purify and cleanse your aura. If you have them, bring a few crystals into your bath, such as clear or smoky quartz or amethyst. Then simply lie back and let the charged water do the work.

Not all crystals should be exposed to water, so do your research beforehand. It is also best to use rounded, polished stones for this. Take care with essential oils and always read the labels.

Sweeping

Sometimes all that is needed is an "energy sweep" in order to cleanse your aura. Sweeping the aura entails calling a purifying energy to the hands. To do this, put your hands comfortably in front of you, with your palms facing up. After a few deep, calming breaths, bring all your attention to your palms. As you breathe in, visualize a bright white light entering your crown and flowing through you. As you breathe out, sense this light reaching your hands and bringing a warm energy to your palms.

When you feel ready, sit upright and bring your hands a few inches above your head. Move your hands around your head and neck in a sweeping motion – over the shoulders, down to the legs and out over the feet. Just above your feet, sweep wide and outwards with a firm gesture. Visualize negative energies dissipating from your aura. Do several sweeps to cover as much of the body outline as possible. This really gives negative energies the brush-off.

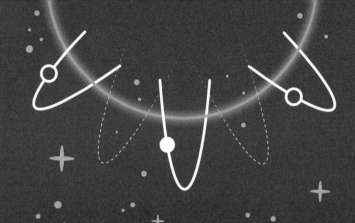

CHAPTER THREE:

RAISE YOUR VIBRATIONS

In the previous chapters we learned about the energy body, and the importance of maintaining a healthy and harmonized energy flow. Now it's time to take things up a notch to help you feel re-energized, reinvigorated and revitalized.

In this chapter, you will find a host of ideas to raise your whole energy vibration. Raising your vibration is all about feeling the energy streams that flow through you and tuning them into joy and happiness. There are techniques here to help you find freedom from negative emotions and feel more in tune with the source of life itself.

✦ RAISE YOUR ENERGY VIBRATION ✦

Raising your energy vibration means:

- ★ Raising your spiritual consciousness.
- ★ Increasing awareness of your energy body.
- ★ Feeling more connected with the abundant cosmic life force that is constantly flowing through your whole being.
- ★ Being more open to regenerative and positive energies.
- ★ Feeling more alive.

To get started, try this exercise to experience the full extent of your aura:

Sit comfortably and relax into a meditative frame of mind with a few deep, relaxing breaths. Focus on your breathing and try to let go of other thoughts. When you are ready, visualize your outer aura as an oval shape surrounding you and extending several feet from your physical outline. Now, with every in-breath, visualize a beam of pure white light entering your crown chakra. Try to sense this light entering the top of your head. With every out-breath, visualize sparkles of pure gold swirling into your aura. Continue until the full extent of your aura is filled with glittering gold!

★ FOUR HEALING QUESTIONS ★

There is a shamanic tradition that when someone visits the shaman in need of healing, they will be asked four questions:

- ★ When did you stop dancing?
- ★ When did you stop singing?
- ★ When did you stop taking joy in stories?
- ★ When was the last time you took comfort in solitude and silence?

These questions can be helpful reminders if our energy has become a little flat and our energy vibration has dropped. With the frenetic pace of modern life, it is easy to forget simple joys. If you need an energy-vibration boost, ask yourself the four simple questions above, and then:

- ★ Put on some music and dance.
- ★ Sing a favourite song at the top of your voice.
- ★ Pick up a favourite book and enjoy a story. Better still, tell a story or, if you feel inspired, write one.
- ★ Take some time out. Set a timer on your phone and just sit still in quiet surroundings for 20 minutes.

✦ CONSUMING COSMIC ENERGY ✦

Whenever we eat, we are consuming cosmic energy. All foodstuffs carry their own vibration and store energy that will be released into our bodies. To maintain a balanced energy flow, it is essential to eat well, and that means not only caring about what we eat, but how we eat.

The energy journey our food undergoes is truly amazing. The humblest of vegetables is the result of an unbroken chain of growing cycles from seed, through soil and to the cooking pot. Through every growth cycle, the energy of the sun has been absorbed and transformed from cosmic rays to carrot, cauliflower, potato or pea. With this in mind, when it is our turn to absorb cosmic energy through eating, it is important to do so with a positive mindset and a receptive heart.

Discover a new relationship with your food using these tips for mindfulness and gratitude:

★ When you bring food into your kitchen, welcome it with thanks. Call to mind abundance and gratitude as you put the food away.

★ For a new awareness of food energy, grow some. Even if it is just a little cress on the windowsill, consuming food you have grown from seed by the light of the sun brings a new sense of energy continuity into your being.

★ Before you eat, raise your vibration by meditating briefly on your connectedness to the source of all cosmic energy. Thank the food you are about to eat and avoid negative conversation at your table; food absorbs all surrounding emotional energies – positive or negative.

★ Eat every mouthful mindfully. Take your time and while you eat, avoid distractions such as your phone or the TV. Welcome the energies that are coming to you, taste everything and enjoy.

★ Treat food as though it is sacred and it will nourish you so much more deeply.

✦ ENERGY-INFUSED WATER ✦

Water is essential to a healthy body and a positive energy flow, and anything that benefits your health can also increase vibrational energy. Water is a remarkable substance, scientifically speaking. The extraordinary chemistry of water ensures that energy is absorbed by all living things, while the unique molecular structure of water ensures that energy flows to all parts of each living being.

Every morning, start your day with energy-infused water – meditate for a moment, with a glass of water in front of you. Begin with a few deep, focused breaths to relax, then spread your hands over the glass and visualize a stream of bright light flowing through your body and into the water. Begin to feel the light energy as perhaps a warm or slight tingling sensation leaving the palms of your hands. Visualize the water glittering and sparkling with light and life. While you drink this water, picture and feel the energy radiating within you, rejuvenating and enlivening your whole being.

✦ FEEL THE EARTH
BENEATH YOUR FEET ✦

Getting out into nature is a powerful way to raise your vibrational energy, and there is nothing quite like the sensation of the Earth beneath your feet. Embrace this wonderful feeling by spending time walking without shoes or socks, sensing the grass, the sand, the soil or just the pavement. This is an effective method to reconnect with the energy of the planet. Feet are naturally sensitive to the sensations of cool grass, hot sand, soft soil or hard pavement. If we wear shoes all the time, we miss out on this direct connection with the Earth.

This lack of connection is like wearing a blindfold. It is so important to take off the blindfold once in a while so that you can discover the "sight" in your feet. Enter a mindful state and notice the Earth's energy flowing up into your body through the soles of your feet, all the time becoming aware of your stability, security and sense of belonging.

✶ EXPERIENCE TREE ENERGY ✶

There is tremendous cosmic energy flowing through trees. While the vibrant energy from the sun surges through all plant life, trees are deeply rooted powerhouses storing decades, and sometimes centuries, of starlight. Trees are bursting with life through the spring to autumn months, yet even in winter they maintain a powerful potential for new life.

It is possible to see the energy field of a tree and witness its aura – an outline of coloured light. To do so, gaze up at a tree's form against the sky when it is in leaf. Take a little time and relax into it. It may be best to try this sitting down, after a few deep, mindful breaths. Allow your whole body to relax, particularly your eyes. Try not to focus on the leaf outline itself, but just beyond it.

After a time, you should start to notice the aura: it will seem just a little lighter than the surrounding sky at first, and quite close to the leaf outline. Sometimes it seems as though faint wisps of grey or purple energy are detectable.

Trees are so generous with their energy. Time spent under the canopy of trees never fails to raise our energy vibration. Try a walk in woodland: move mindfully among the trees, particularly when leaves are abundant. Become aware of the leaf canopy as you walk and the vibrant array of greens. Think of yourself as bathing, submerged beneath an "energy sea". Notice how the leaf canopy ripples with sunlight.

Stroll slowly between the trees and spread your hands on their bark. Remind yourself that just like you, trees have an energy-field aura. As you move from tree to tree, become aware that you are passing between energy auras. As your aura blends with that of each tree, try to maintain an openness and generosity of being. Allow your vibration to resonate and harmonize with that which flows from the trees around you, in order to receive the abundant living energy.

✷ TAPPING THE ENERGY ✷

One way to release an energy block or circulate better quality vibrational energy within the body is through a practice called the Emotional Freedom Technique, or EFT. This is particularly effective for those who find it difficult to tune into the energy that flows through them. This is because it relies on a sequence of tapping – by the fingertips of one hand – on nine specific areas of the physical body known as "meridian points". In this way, a circuit of energy sensation is built up which allows anyone to literally feel the flow.

EFT (or simply "tapping") depends on an awareness of the energy circuits that run throughout the body. These are the same energy circuits that lie at the heart of acupuncture and acupressure. Tapping can help reduce stress and anxiety, but more fundamentally, it sets up healing energy cycles and elevates the vibrations in your body.

★ PREPARING TO TAP ★

★ Before you start tapping, identify what you would like to focus on. Think about the areas in your life that are causing you difficulty. It could be a situation or issue that is creating anxiety, or an energy block making it difficult for you to move forward and flourish.

★ How do you feel about the issue or blockage now? Rate your feelings about the area of concern from 0–10, with 10 being the highest intensity. This might be the level of anxiety, frustration or hurt.

★ Decide on a "set-up" statement. The set-up statement helps you acknowledge the problem, and then invite acceptance. This helps dissipate any self-judgement from the healing process. Example set-up statements might be:

"Even though I am anxious about my work, I accept these feelings."

"Although I cannot seem to release this hurt, I accept who I am."

✦ WHERE TO TAP ✦

Below is the name and location for each meridian point, listed in tapping order:

Karate Chop (KC): The outer edge of the hand between the bottom of the little finger and the wrist.
Eyebrow Point (EB): Where the eyebrow meets the bridge of the nose.
Side of Eye (SE): On the bone of the eye socket, on the outer side of the eye.
Under Eye (UE): On the top centre of the cheekbone, immediately under the eye.
Under Nose (UN): Directly beneath the nose, above the upper lip.
Chin Point (CP): Just below the bottom lip and above the chin.
Collarbone Point (CB): On the collarbone, in alignment with the side of the neck.
Under Arm (UA): On the side of the body, around 4 inches under the armpit.
Top of Head (TH): On the very top of the head, on the crown.

✦ HOW TO TAP ✦

Tapping is done with the fingers of one hand, around six times, at each of the nine meridian points in turn.

★ Sitting in a comfortable upright position, ensure you can easily reach and locate each of the meridian points. You will need to be able to tap directly on the collarbone and underarm, which might not be easy if you are wearing too many layers.

★ Take a few deep breaths to relax.

★ Starting with the Karate Chop, tap around six times on the side of the hand while you recite your set-up statement.

★ Work your way through the remaining eight points, tapping softly. Take care around your eyes. As you move on from each point, you should experience no more than a light tingling sensation. While tapping at each point, repeat a phrase addressing the issue or blockage you'd like to work on, for example: "Let go of anxiety", or "Release my hurt".

★ TAPPING CYCLES ★

Tapping can be usefully completed through a few cycles per session. At the end of each sequence, it is helpful to pause and assess how you feel before beginning another cycle:

★ When you complete a tapping sequence, take a deep relaxing breath or two. How do you feel about your issue or blockage now? Can you sense the flow of a healing energy? Just as you did at the start, rate the intensity of your issue or blockage. Have you noticed a change?

★ Complete another tapping sequence if you would like to further reduce the intensity of any negative feelings and increase healing energy flow.

★ Each time you prepare for a new tapping sequence, adapt your set-up statement. It is important that you release any potential judgement. For example:

"Even though I am still anxious about my work, I welcome the healing to come."

"Although the hurt remains, I give myself time to heal."

✦ WATCH A SUNRISE ✦

The sun is the source of all energy on Earth and, in common with all stars, it is a massive concentration of the cosmic energy that fills the universe. Every morning since the dawn of our planet, the daily miracle of sunrise has taken place. Not only is watching a sunrise calming and stress-relieving, it can also help raise your vibration frequency.

Sometime between late spring and mid-autumn, on a day you don't have to rush, wake up an hour or so before sunrise and go somewhere special to enjoy it. From a hill, you can look to the horizon and watch the light gradually grow. From a shore, you can watch the sea take on a scattering of glitter. Ensure you don't stare directly at the sun but take time to enjoy the sounds of nature awakening and feel the warmth of morning. The refreshing energy of renewal will rejuvenate and intensify your energy flow.

✦ FIND TIME FOR PLAY ✦

For many people, growing older means they stop playing. And yet, when it comes to raising our vibration and welcoming regenerative energies, the lively excitement and simple wonder of a child playing freely is exactly what we need. Let's face it, children never seem to run out of energy for play.

Try these playtime ideas to welcome some rejuvenating energy, and rediscover your childlike joy:

Go to the beach
Remember running close to the sea then trying to run away from a wave? Or building a sandcastle with a moat filled with seawater? Spend some time at the beach and don't just rest, play!

Have an adventure
Take a walk in the woods and let your imagination do the rest. Search for fairy houses or make a den from sticks and leaves.

Fly a kite
Go out on a windy day and have fun trying to keep a kite in the air. It's never easy, but it's always fun!

✦ VISIT A LIMINAL PLACE ✦

Cosmic energy is liveliest at the borders of things, in liminal spaces. This is where energy is given and received between energy centres.

Many of the most famous sacred spaces are liminal, for example, ancient burial grounds, because they represent the border between the living and their ancestors from the past. Stonehenge, in Wiltshire, England, is another example, representing a circle of doorways, each a threshold of liminality.

Ancient Celtic wisdom found that the edge of water at a lake or river had a powerful, liminal energy. This was felt particularly in autumn, as the mist would rise between the Earth and the water. Here, the blended borders may have given them insight into connectedness and oneness. Time spent at any shore, whether river, lake or ocean, is always refreshing and offers the insight of energy in perpetual motion, both giving and receiving.

In everyday life, an accessible liminal space might be a doorway, at the edge of a body of water, or even a train station or airport. But just being outside, at one with nature, can improve mood, lower stress levels and raise vibrational energy.

✦ DECLUTTER AND DETOX ✦

Our vibrational energies are easily affected by our environment, and the most significant environment for most of us is our home. Home has a special resonance in our energy systems, even if it isn't always the place we spend most of our time. Our home is related to our core identity, so it is an energy we always carry with us. Therefore, it needs to be the place where we renew and replenish, where we rest our bodies and restore our well-being. Even thinking about home can help us do this, so it is always good energy practice to take care of our home environment.

Try these steps to declutter and detox your home in order to unblock energies and clear out toxins:

★ The Bathroom: Clear out all those gels, creams, bottles and jars you don't use. Aim to keep a smaller range of simpler products. Focus on natural ingredients for soaps and shampoos where possible and be gentle on the planet where you can.

★ The Kitchen: Are all those cleaning products really necessary, and could they be contributing to the toxins in your home? Get rid of any you don't need and consider replacing harsh chemicals with kinder alternatives. Distilled vinegar and bicarbonate of soda are excellent cleaners, with no toxicity. Also think about disposing of any BPA plastics you may still have.

★ The Living Areas: Is dust gathering on bookshelves and surfaces? Is the energy of your living area dominated by technology? Have a clear-out of unwanted books and ornaments. Try arranging furniture to make entertainment technology an option rather than the centre of attention.

★ The Bedroom: Bedrooms should be temples of rest and sleep. Consider keeping technology out of the bedroom by setting up a phone-charging point outside the room. This will encourage you to leave your mobile on the threshold as you enter your bedroom at night.

✦ TAKE A BREAK FROM THE NEWS ✦

The news can become a constant negative narrative in our lives. News media is rarely uplifting and much of the time the compelling nature of it is found in its relentless reporting of impending doom. News narratives tend to dwell on the worst sides of human nature, which influences how we see others. What's more, media messaging has never been more insistent: bulletins pop up minute by minute on our phones and browsers.

Take a break in order to break the cycle of doom. Plan a week without news by switching off or blocking any news content. Listen to music in the car instead, and find something uplifting to watch in place of news on the TV. It isn't easy to avoid but a few days off can really help reset your sense of perspective. It can also provide a chance to welcome subtler positive energies, which are all too easily drowned out by the intrusive narratives of fear, so that you can tune into a higher vibrational frequency.

★ LISTEN TO CLASSICAL MUSIC ★

How long has it been since you listened to a piece of classical music all the way through? Studies have shown classical music is linked to many health benefits, including stress relief, boosted brain power and improved sleep, making it the perfect way to experience high-frequency living.

Classical music is experienced in layers of sound, from duets to full orchestras. At its heart, the music is pure energy, which works through a range of frequencies, vibrations and harmonics.

Try listening to a complete piece of classical music, fully relaxed, perhaps with your eyes closed. Avoid all other distractions and really pay attention. Here are a few uplifting pieces to try:

★ "Violin Sonata No. 17 in C" – Wolfgang Amadeus Mozart

★ "Classical Symphony" – Sergei Prokofiev

★ "Ruslan and Ludmila (Overture)" – Mikhail Glinka

★ "Jupiter the Bringer of Jollity" (*The Planets*) – Gustav Holst

★ "Spring Symphony" (Allegro) – Robert Schumann

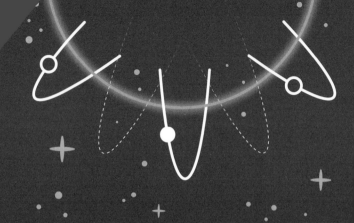

CHAPTER FOUR:

MANIFEST
POSITIVE ENERGY

Having explored our true nature as beings of pure energy, we have seen how important it is to look after our energy self and maintain a positive, life-enriching vibration.

In this chapter, we will learn how to work with our cosmic energy to bring our hopes and dreams to fruition. We will find a practical formula to harness our energy streams in order to manifest our goals, allowing us to flourish. Our energy flow has always been seeking our happiness and fulfilment: this is how to go with it and let it happen.

✳ ASK, GIVE, BELIEVE AND RECEIVE ✳

In Chapter One, we saw how our cosmic energy can be usefully understood as four streams of one light. These are the active, responsive, reflective and receptive energies. These streams are interdependent but they each illuminate an aspect of the energy self. The four streams of energy align appropriately with the core principles of manifestation: ask, give, believe and receive.

"Ask, give, believe and receive" is a formula for success when bringing anything to fruition with the support of cosmic energy. Asking requires your active energy, giving requires your responsive energy, believing requires your reflective energy, and receiving requires your receptive energy.

As we will see over the next few pages, this formula works with two important energy manifestation principles: the power of intention and the laws of attraction (the idea that positive thoughts and actions reap positive rewards, and vice versa for negative ones). In a sense, this formula is a tuning dial to help you adjust your cosmic frequency towards welcoming good things into your life and the lives of those around you.

★ ASK ★

Realizing your goals requires you to first be very clear about what your goals are. Asking involves forming a positive intention and empowering it with positive motivation; for this, it is necessary to channel inspiration and enthusiasm.

The intention arises from deep within who you are – your desires combined with your spiritual purpose. To allow an intention to arise is to be inspired towards your life's goal. To give an intention energy requires enthusiasm.

Inspiration and enthusiasm therefore provide the momentum to empower your intentions. When you can draw your intention from inspiration and envision it with enthusiasm, you can ask for anything with confidence and excitement.

★ EFFECTIVE ASKING ★

To live by the principles of positive manifestation, our first maxim is disarmingly simple: "Ask, and you will receive." There is a powerful energy of confidence and belief behind this and it can leave us wondering if it is that easy, why don't we just ask? However, there may be many reasons why we don't. Perhaps we lack confidence, or think we are undeserving of greater happiness, or maybe we don't want to appear ungrateful for what we already have. These sorts of difficulties can block positive manifestation from the outset.

Asking should be as straightforward as it sounds. Avoid self-limiting thoughts and know that the universe wants you to flourish. Effective asking follows four basic steps:

★ Know what to ask for
★ Actually ask for it
★ Align all your energies with your request
★ Transform your request into empowered intention

Let's take a look at each of these four steps and turn your dreams into intentions!

Knowing what to ask for

Knowing what to ask for can be surprisingly difficult. If you're stuck, unblock your third-eye chakra (see Chapter Two) to encourage clarity and open your intuition, or try this meditative exercise to activate inspiration:

★ Enter a calm, mindful and relaxed mode of awareness: with eyes closed, take time to breathe deeply and concentrate only on your breath for a time. You can draw on your active energy stream by simply asking for inspiration. Recite a phrase a few times over, such as, "Help me see the best in me." Visualize and try to sense your active energy filling your being like light. Relax in this energy and welcome any images or thoughts that arise.

★ When you finish the meditation, take a journal and write freely about "future you". You might gravitate to poetry form, a diary entry or a mind map. Read over your notes and circle the clearest expression of your primary goal, desire or need. Use this to frame your request.

Actually asking

Once you are clear what to ask for to enrich your life and support you towards flourishing, you need to actually ask. This sets up your request with clarity and provides you with a precise focal point for your energy and enthusiasm.

The first step to asking is to write your request in a succinct sentence. Phrase it in a reasonably open way and remember: cosmic abundance wants you to achieve your dreams, and cosmic potential is limitless. This means you can ask for anything in confidence, but it should ultimately serve your highest good.

For example, "I ask cosmic abundance for a huge lottery win" may reflect a strong desire, but may not serve your highest good. In effect, this places limits on cosmic energy, which in turn compromises results. A better alternative is, "I welcome financial wealth into my life." This can be fulfilled in a way that supports both your spiritual growth and your financial needs.

Align your energies to your request

Each time you think about your request, you give it energy. Your thoughts are pure energy, just as you are, and they will ultimately manifest in some form or other. They can manifest as your realized goals and desires, or as the person you become. If your request is to present itself positively, it needs to be given constructive energy in your thoughts. However, unless all of your energy streams are aligned favourably towards your goal, one or other of them may block, delay or negatively impact manifestation.

Use these energy-stream affirmations when your thoughts turn to your requests, goals and dreams:

- ★ Active Affirmation: I am excited and working towards... [your request].
- ★ Responsive Affirmation: My heart is open and my arms embrace... [your request].
- ★ Reflective Affirmation: I am loved by the universe and deserve... [your request].
- ★ Receptive Affirmation: I give thanks to abundance for... [your request].

Transform requests into empowered intentions

Requests are like wishes – they are somewhat unstable and built in uncertainty. When you wish for things, they tend to stay wishes – just fantasies to pass the time and stretch the imagination. Requests have the option of being turned down. It's not that the cosmic abundance turns down requests as such, it's just that you are an important part of fulfilling your own requests, and if you think of them as optional, they might remain unrealized. It is important, therefore, to transform your requests into empowered intentions.

Try the 777 manifestation technique, which entails some journaling. Three times a day, find a few moments to work on transforming your request or goal. During these brief sessions, write your request or goal down seven times, say it aloud to yourself seven times, and repeat it inwardly in your heart seven times. That way your requests and goals will become empowered intentions on paper, in your mind and in your heart.

✦ GIVE ✦

Following the principles of positive manifestation, the second maxim is: "In order to receive, give." The implication is that when you give, you will be generously rewarded with abundance. This is a universal spiritual law expressed as *karma* in some Hindu and Buddhist traditions, or as the three-fold law in Wicca and some neopagan spiritualities. The three-fold law finds that the energy you give will return back to you threefold; three times the positive energies, but also three times the negative. Giving to receive very much underpins the laws of attraction that are key to manifestation (see overleaf).

Giving requires the generosity of spirit and open-heartedness that arises in your responsive energies. Once you have formed and empowered your intentions, it is important to remember that you are pure energy, inseparably connected with all other energies. The more you give in your daily energy transactions, the more you will receive to energize and realize your intentions.

★ GIVING AND THE LAWS OF ATTRACTION ★

When cosmic energy brings things to fruition, it does so following three laws of attraction:

Like attracts like

This law says that the energies you send out will be the energies that flow back to you. If you send out positive, expansive, generous energies, you will find you receive the same in return. Think of this process as an amplification loop: send out energies of growth and they will help you grow.

Energy is constantly renewed

When you give energy, you do not deplete yourself, you renew yourself. The insights of the universal, infinitely connected energy field prove this. There are no gaps in the field, just countless energy transactions giving and receiving between centres of light.

There is only now

Energy is never lost, and you don't need to store it. There is no past or future, just an eternal now. This means we can give without reserve and shine a little brighter in the forever now.

How to give

To live is to give, and to give is to live. Most of us these days live in commodified, consumerist societies in which true selflessness and unreserved giving are radical ideas. We have been conditioned to believe that resources are scarce, and that we are all in competition with each other for the essentials and pleasures of life. The truth is that – in cosmic energy terms – there are no limits, and no competition: the more we give, the more there is. Giving can be done across the four energy streams:

★ Active Giving: Share your enthusiasm with others and for others. Inspire others when you can and be excited for their goals.

★ Responsive Giving: Give time to others, be as open as you can and truly listen. Break your heart open and don't fear hurt.

★ Reflective Giving: Be kind to yourself and forgive yourself the mistakes of the past.

★ Receptive Giving: Allow others to give to you and accept their support and love.

⋆ BELIEVE ⋆

The third maxim of positive manifestation is: "Believe it, and it will happen." This statement shows the limitless power of belief. Belief is like a secret magic our ancestors have been encoding in folk tales and myths for as long as there have been stories to tell. So often, the hero of these stories has their belief tested and must discover or rediscover it in order to restore harmony and goodness. On many occasions it is the simple belief of a child or the childlike that is the most powerful.

Our conviction that our dreams can come true is so often flattened by our interactions in the world. Cynicism is such a common mindset that we discourage each other with phrases like, "I'm just being realistic." Be ready to sweep away cynicism and pessimism – no energy is ever wasted and the universe will reward every effort. Make that start, take that first step. Let others be "realistic" while you make something real!

Self-Belief

Our belief draws from our reflective energy stream and is the bedrock of realizing intentions. Realization is a powerful word when it comes to intentions. To realize is to take an idea and make it tangible.

For many of us, our goals, dreams and intentions are very much focused on who we are and who we would like to be, which is itself tied up with how we see ourselves and how we think others see us. Believing therefore starts with self-belief. We cannot secure confident belief in the universe until we have some confident belief in ourselves.

To begin strengthening your self-belief, switch off doubt in your self-talk and conversation:

- ★ Switch "if" to "when": "If I am successful..." becomes "When I am successful..."
- ★ Switch "when" to "now": "When I feel ready..." becomes "Now I feel ready..."
- ★ Switch "should" to "shall": "I should..." becomes "I shall..."

★ CREATIVE VISUALIZATION ★

One of the most powerful tools to strengthen belief and realize your intentions is creative visualization. Many professional athletes use this technique to positively charge and improve their performance. Simply visualizing a successful outcome energizes an intention and builds it up as a reality in the mind. The more we play out positive outcomes in the situations we face, the more real they become in our minds and the more we come to believe in them as real possibilities. Soon, real possibilities are transformed into possible realities.

The Butterfly Bloom

The Butterfly Bloom is a creative visualization technique that you can use to empower your goals and intentions with creative energy. The energy of your imagination becomes transformed and amplified into an energy of manifestation.

★ Sit comfortably, close your eyes and relax with a few deep, mindful breaths.

★ When you are ready, picture something in your mind that you would like to manifest.

Take time to imagine this as clearly as possible. Picture this goal or intention as though it has already happened. Place yourself there, receiving or achieving your goal. Feel the joy and gratitude fill your entire being.

★ In your mind's eye, surround this imagining with a pink glow. Pink is a colour associated with the heart chakra, so breathe into your heart as you visualize your goal or intention glowing brightly with pink light. Feel the energy surrounding your goal or intention intensify.

★ Now all you have to do is release the energy out into the cosmic energy field. When you are ready, simply imagine your goal or intention with its positive feelings of success bursting into a bloom of beautiful pink butterflies. Picture thousands of butterflies fluttering in all directions carrying your goal or intention, each one gathering more and more energy towards fruition.

★ There is nothing else to do. Finish the visualization and give thanks.

✦ RECEIVE ✦

Receiving draws from our receptive energy stream and is the final step in the manifestation formula. It should also be the easiest part of the process: a simple, passive matter of accepting what cosmic abundance has prepared for you. This leads us to the fourth and final maxim of positive manifestation: "Only the open can be filled." The spirit of this statement is that to receive, you need to be receptive.

Keep in mind that receiving can be, should be and will be a simple joy. You might need to recalibrate your receptive energies a little, but the energy you are tuning into is that of the excited and unquestioning child. This is an energy of trust, hope, anticipation and wonder. Above all, it is pure, simple and unambiguous.

Preparing to Receive

Receiving abundant cosmic energy should be like standing in a downpour of summer rain. Imagine that after a few long, hot weeks of scorching sun, you know without a doubt that it is about to rain. Others around you are incredulous and shake their heads, but they don't look up like you do. You stand with arms open wide and expectant face turned to the sky. As the first heavy, cool drops fall on your face, it feels so exhilarating. Then, as others still refuse to see it, the drops turn into a downpour, leaving you refreshed and invigorated, full of joy.

There will always be those who will not fully receive the abundant energy of life, and sometimes their energies will act to limit yours. Choose to remain as receptive as possible to life through these four basic principles:

* ★ Awareness
* ★ Openness
* ★ Self-Worth
* ★ Gratitude

Let's take a look at these four principles in turn and get ready to receive abundance!

★ AWARENESS ★

Raising your awareness is key to expanding your receptive energies. This is simply about noticing things more than usual. These days we're often so busy rushing to the next thing we barely notice the here and now. Try slowing down a little and letting good things come to you rather than chasing after them. Take some time each day to live in the present moment and practise some mindfulness; it will really open up your receptive energies. If the universe is trying to tell you something, be ready to listen.

Try a walk of the senses

Go for a wander somewhere local without a planned destination or time limit and switch your phone off. As you walk, give yourself the opportunity to notice – really notice – things you might normally overlook. Think about all your senses as you do this. Observe the familiar with fresh eyes, listen for different sounds or pay attention to smells and textures.

⋆ OPENNESS ⋆

How do you feel about a fresh start, a new you or a chance to break out of your routine? Much of the time we say we would like to try something different or to seize an exciting opportunity, but when it really comes down to it, we tend to just stick with the safe and familiar. There's nothing wrong with the way things are if you are finding fulfilment and happiness, but it is often the case that we resist the very change we want for ourselves.

It is natural to fear the unknown, and change always invites this. Becoming more open to change is key to rejuvenating your receptive energies.

★ SELF-WORTH ★

When it comes to our receptive energies, how we see ourselves is highly significant. Self-image, self-respect and our sense of self-worth can all influence our willingness to accept what cosmic abundance has in store for us. To maintain a receptive mode, it is important that our sense of self is balanced and sensitive. Self-worth is essentially the pride we have in ourselves; too little of this and we regard ourselves as unworthy of cosmic goodness. Too much and we reject anything that looks like charity, believing we must depend only on ourselves.

Practise self-kindness

We are often much kinder to others than we are to ourselves. Try a journaling exercise for self-kindness. Think of yourself as a friend who has come to you for advice. What advice is your friend looking for? How will you help your friend? Write this down as a dialogue and be as kind to your new friend as you can.

✦ GRATITUDE ✦

Adopting a thankful outlook to life is so rewarding, and it tends to be the difference between those who are happy now and those who are not happy yet; thankfulness brings cosmic abundance into the now, rather than the not yet. For as long as you are waiting to give thanks, you will be waiting to accept good things; gratitude also helps with receptive awareness. It is a painful truth that we don't always appreciate what we have while we're chasing around for something else.

Thank the morning

Each morning, give thanks for a new day, creating a springboard for your ongoing mood. To achieve this, take note of the very first thought that enters your mind as you wake and practise mindfulness at this time until your first thought is automatically a thankful one.

★ ASK, GIVE, BELIEVE THEN RECEIVE OVERFLOW ★

Back in Chapter One, we saw how one small change in our active, responsive, reflective and receptive energies may be all it takes to set up a kind of feedforward loop of energy resonance. Once one energy stream begins to flow with greater vitality, it will feed another, which in turn will feed another until our whole selves are overflowing with positive energy. The ask, give, believe and receive formula is aligned with the four streams of the energy self and works in exactly the same way. This means that a small change in one part of the formula will feed the others, leading to abundance overflow.

For example, if you are wrestling with self-confidence, you may struggle to believe that anything good will come to you. Perhaps you don't consider yourself important enough for some reason. Cosmic abundance doesn't agree, and is looking for any opportunity to give you everything you need to flourish and feel joy. The trouble is, if you do struggle with self-confidence, this may be the one thing you would like to ask for from cosmic abundance, but paradoxically you lack the confidence to ask.

The good news is that cosmic abundance only needs you to start up the feedforward loop and it will take care of the rest. So if you are struggling in this way, leave asking and believing for a while, and make a start with giving and receiving. Look for new opportunities to positively give to others in kindness, and prepare to receive with thankfulness. Soon you will feel able to form your request and believe in your intentions.

Remember – the feedforward loop is built into cosmic energy manifestation, so however empty you feel right now, prepare for overflow!

⭑ CONCLUSION ⭑

At the beginning of this book, we saw how the universe – and everything in it – is pure cosmic energy. We realized all this energy exists as a potentially infinite, interconnected field, like a vast sea of light, and understood each of us exists as our own energy being within this sea. With respect to our energy bodies, we have identified the energy streams that flow continuously to, through and from us, and how we live in an energetic relationship with all other living beings, continually giving and receiving. We have learned our energy bodies are regulated through seven chakras, and that we radiate beyond our physical form as seven auric bodies.

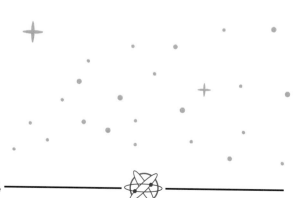

Now you have these empowering insights, you can be in control of your own energies, employing them to achieve your goals, realize your true self and manifest your dreams more fully. You are free to liberate yourself from negative thought patterns, sweep away unhelpful emotional attachments and release that self-restricting mindset. So, go ahead and welcome the regenerative and abundant forces of cosmic energy and allow yourself to flourish.

THE LITTLE BOOK REIKI
Stephanie Drane

ISBN: 978-1-80007-684-6

Discover the benefits of reiki

Reiki is a Japanese complementary therapy with the aim of bringing balance and well-being to the body, mind and spirit. Drawing on the energy of the universe, it seeks to direct and apply this life force to restore health and harmony in the individual.

Step into the world of reiki and find out how you can tap into the energy around you and use it to nurture and nourish yourself physically, emotionally and spiritually.

THE LITTLE BOOK OF MANIFESTATION
Astrid Carvel

ISBN: 978-1-80007-262-6

It's time to start changing your life

The universe is ready to give you what you want, if you're willing to make the right moves.

This beginner's guide is here to explain what manifesting is, how it works, and the simple steps you can take to get started. Based on the law of attraction and the principle of visualization, the core methods and techniques in this book will help you identify and progress towards your goals, and maintain the momentum once you get going.

Have you enjoyed this book?
If so, find us on Facebook at **Summersdale Publishers**, on Twitter at **@Summersdale** and on Instagram and TikTok at **@summersdalebooks** and get in touch. We'd love to hear from you!

www.summersdale.com

Image credits

p.30 – frequency waves © Theus/Shutterstock.com;
pp.36–38 – chakras © MaddyZ/Shutterstock.com